BRACHIOSAURUS

by Bradley Cole

Cody Koala
An Imprint of Pop!
popbooksonline.com

abdobooks.com
Published by Pop!, a division of ABDO, PO Box 398166, Minneapolis, Minnesota 55439.

Printed in the United States of America, North Mankato, Minnesota.

082018
012019

THIS BOOK CONTAINS RECYCLED MATERIALS

Cover Photo: iStockphoto
Interior Photos: iStockphoto, 1, 12, 21; Kim Taylor / Warren Photographic/ Science Source, 5; Joe Tucciarone/Science Source, 7; Mark Hallett Paleoart/ Science Source, 8; Science Picture Co/Science Source, 11; Millard H. Sharp/ Science Source, 15 (top); Eckehard Schulz/AP Images, 15 (bottom left); Shutterstock Images, 15 (bottom right), 16, 19

Editor: Meg Gaertner
Series Designer: Laura Mitchell

Library of Congress Control Number: 2018949752

Publisher's Cataloging-in-Publication Data
Names: Cole, Bradley, author.
Title: Brachiosaurus / by Bradley Cole.
Description: Minneapolis, Minnesota : Pop!, 2019 | Series: Dinosaurs | Includes online resources and index.
Identifiers: ISBN 9781532161780 (lib. bdg.) | ISBN 9781641855495 (pbk) | ISBN 9781532162848 (ebook)
Subjects: LCSH: Brachiosaurus--Juvenile literature. | Dinosaurs--Juvenile literature. | Extinct animals--Juvenile literature.
Classification: DDC 567.914--dc23

Hello! My name is

Cody Koala

Pop open this book and you'll find QR codes like this one, loaded with information, so you can learn even more!

Scan this code* and others like it while you read, or visit the website below to make this book pop.

popbooksonline.com/brachiosaurus

*Scanning QR codes requires a web-enabled smart device with a QR code reader app and a camera.

Table of Contents

Chapter 1

Giant Dinosaur

Brachiosaurus was a plant-eating dinosaur. It lived in **herds** during the **Jurassic Period**. This was about 150 million years ago.

Watch a video here!

Chapter 2

Arm Lizard

The name Brachiosaurus means "arm lizard." The dinosaur's front legs were much longer than its back legs.

Learn more here!

Brachiosaurus stood as tall as a four-story building. It had a very long neck. It could reach high branches in trees.

Brachiosaurus had a short, strong tail. Its tail probably helped it balance.

Brachiosaurus had a huge **nasal cavity** on top of its head. Because of it, scientists used to think the dinosaur lived in the water. **Nostrils** on top of its head would have helped it breathe while swimming.

large nasal cavity
long neck
shorter back legs
longer front legs

Now scientists believe the dinosaur lived on flat land. They believe its nostrils were at the front of its head. These nostrils helped the dinosaur smell. They helped it maintain its own body temperature.

Chapter 3

Plant Eater

Brachiosaurus had teeth shaped like spoons. These helped it pull leaves from branches.

Complete an activity here!

Brachiosaurus could not chew food. It could only open and close its mouth. It swallowed its food whole.

Brachiosaurus spent most of its day eating.

Chapter 4

Fossil Clues

Brachiosaurus **fossils** have been found in Europe, North America, and Africa. Complete **skeletons** have been found.

Learn more here!

Most of the fossils belong to young Brachiosaurus. The dinosaur could have grown to be even bigger. Brachiosaurus was one of the largest land animals ever.

Baggage Claim
Animal Relief Area

Making Connections

Text-to-Self

Brachiosaurus ate leaves from the tops of trees. What vegetables do you like to eat?

Text-to-Text

Have you read books about other dinosaurs? How are those dinosaurs similar to or different from Brachiosaurus?

Text-to-World

Brachiosaurus used its long neck to reach its food. How do other animals use parts of their body to eat?

Glossary

fossil – the remains of a plant or an animal from a long time ago.

herd – a large group of animals that live and travel together.

Jurassic Period – a period that lasted from about 200 million years ago to about 145 million years ago.

nasal cavity – the inside of the nose.

nostril – one of two openings to the nose that animals use to smell and to breathe in air.

skeleton – the bones that support the body.

Index

Online Resources

popbooksonline.com

Thanks for reading this Cody Koala book!

Scan this code* and others like it in this book, or visit the website below to make this book pop!

popbooksonline.com/brachiosaurus

*Scanning QR codes requires a web-enabled smart device with a QR code reader app and a camera.